CALIFORNIA'S
GOLD RUSH

CALIFORNIA'S
GOLD RUSH
BY ROBERT GRAYSON

Content Consultant
Eric Morser, assistant professor of American history
Skidmore College

ABDO
Publishing Company

CREDITS

Published by ABDO Publishing Company, PO Box 398166, Minneapolis, MN 55439. Copyright © 2012 by Abdo Consulting Group, Inc. International copyrights reserved in all countries. No part of this book may be reproduced in any form without written permission from the publisher. The Essential Library™ is a trademark and logo of ABDO Publishing Company.

Printed in the United States of America, North Mankato, Minnesota
092011
012012

 THIS BOOK CONTAINS AT LEAST 10% RECYCLED MATERIALS.

Editor: Paula Lewis
Copy Editor: Rebecca Rowell
Interior Design and Production: Marie Tupy
Cover Design: Kazuko Collins

Library of Congress Cataloging-in-Publication Data
Grayson, Robert, 1951-
  California's Gold Rush / Robert Grayson.
     p. cm. -- (Essential events)
  Includes bibliographical references and index.
  ISBN 978-1-61783-096-9
  1. California--Gold discoveries--Juvenile literature. 2. Gold mines and mining--California--History--19th century--Juvenile literature. 3. Frontier and pioneer life--California--Juvenile literature. 4. California--History--1846-1850--Juvenile literature. 5. California--History--1850-1950--Juvenile literature. I. Title.
  F865.G735 2012
  979.4'04--dc22
                                        2011007941

TABLE OF CONTENTS

James Marshall found gold in January 1848.

EUREKA!

or most people living in the western United States in the mid-1800s, finding gold was only a wild dream, a fanciful myth fueled by rumor, speculation, and tall tales. The most skeptical were those born and raised in the East who chose to move to the West for the adventure of settling a new and untamed land. They were more likely to brush aside stories of untold riches in the ground than those who hailed from California and Nevada.

James Wilson Marshall was a carpenter from New Jersey and one of those skeptics. Yet, on a January morning in 1848, Marshall became a believer as he spotted traces of the glittering precious metal in a narrow channel in central California. That sighting set off one of the most far-reaching events in US history—the California gold rush. Drawn by the lure of quick riches, thousands of people took a risk and swarmed to the West. The influx of settlers prompted the creation of new forms of transportation and new businesses to meet the demands of the miners.

But there were other sides to the gold rush as well. As California's population quickly soared to 90,000 citizens, it sought immediate statehood.

A Modest Gold Rush

On March 9, 1842, six years before Marshall's discovery, rancher Francisco Lopez was herding cattle on his niece's ranch in Placerita Canyon. The ranch was located 35 miles (56 km) northwest of a small town with a population of approximately 1,600 people. It was called Los Angeles. In the afternoon, Lopez stopped by a creek to pick some wild onions for his wife. When he pulled the onions from the ground, he noticed some yellow particles clinging to the roots. The gold he found that day touched off a modest local gold rush. For the next six years, the quarry where Lopez picked those onions yielded 125 pounds (57 kg) of gold. This find was much smaller than Marshall's in 1848.

California's proposed state constitution prohibited slavery so free labor was not in competition for jobs. Once again, Americans had to deal with the issue of slavery. After debates and compromises, California was propelled to statehood in 1850 as a free state.

From East to West

Raised in Lambertville, New Jersey, Marshall had some schooling while learning his father's trade of carpentry. In 1834, at the age of 24, Marshall decided to follow the lead of many other young people and headed out West. At the time, the Missouri River delineated the West from the East. After plying his trade in Indiana and Illinois for ten years, he moved west of the Missouri River to Kansas and farmed for several years.

Farming was hard work. Like many who toiled for long hours in the field, Marshall became a victim of disease. He contracted malaria and was told by a doctor to seek out a drier climate farther west. Marshall left Missouri in 1845 for Oregon and took up carpentry once again. Restless, Marshall ventured south later that year. In search of work and a new mission in life, Marshall traveled to California, which was a Mexican possession at the time.

CAPTAIN SUTTER

Johann August Sutter emigrated from Switzerland to the United States in 1834. Once he arrived, he began using the name John Augustus Sutter. Over the next five years, he traveled extensively to areas such as Oregon, Vancouver, and Alaska. In 1839, he settled in California, a Mexican province, and became a Mexican citizen. He met members of the Mexican elite by introducing himself as Captain John Sutter of the Swiss Guard. While Sutter had served in the Swiss military, there was no evidence that he ever reached any

California Dreaming

When Sutter came to the United States in 1834, he was escaping from creditors in Switzerland. Business dealings that had gone sour left him in substantial debt, so he abandoned his wife and five children in search of riches in the New World. He arrived in New York by ship in July 1834 and headed to Saint Louis, Missouri, where there were job opportunities. In Saint Louis, Sutter became a merchant and an innkeeper. But a farmer at heart, he had a dream of starting an agricultural community.

Hearing about the wide-open spaces in California, Sutter decided that was the place for him. Knowing he would need to gain favor with the Mexican authorities who ran California, Sutter purchased a military uniform before leaving Saint Louis. He then made his way to the small town of Yerba Buena (now San Francisco) in 1839. He wore the uniform to enhance his image as Captain Sutter. Mexican authorities were duly impressed. Once he received his land grant in California's Central Valley, Sutter continued to wear the uniform and became the local legend he had created.

rank near that of captain. Nevertheless, from that time on, he was referred to with the highest regard as Captain.

Mexican government officials were impressed with Sutter and gave him a land grant in 1841 of 48,827 acres (19,760 ha) in central California. The land was exceptionally fertile, and he began building an agricultural settlement and trading post. The huge tract of land was known as Sutter's Fort, which he called New Helvetia. It would become the center of the city of Sacramento.

THE VIRTUES OF A SAWMILL

Eventually, Marshall made his way to Sutter's Fort in the Sacramento valley. In July 1845, Marshall began working for Sutter. He made everything from looms and spinning wheels to tools and furniture, providing services that Sutter's agricultural community sorely needed. Marshall was an accomplished carpenter and a reliable worker. He convinced Sutter in early 1847 to build a sawmill to serve the lumber needs of the fort. By doing so, Sutter could cut his own lumber instead of buying costly lumber in San Francisco and having it brought to New Helvetia.

John Sutter

Marshall looked for the perfect spot for the mill. It had to be close to a river that was big enough to power the mill and transport lumber by water to the fort. The mill also had to be far enough away from the river so a flood would not destroy it.

After weeks of searching, Marshall found a piece of land that was suited for a mill. It was located about 45 miles (73 km) northeast of the fort and near the American River in Coloma. Sutter agreed that the site was ideal. By late August 1847, work had begun on the mill.

Marshall was the foreman for the construction project and would oversee the mill once it was in operation. In his agreement with Sutter, Marshall would be paid for his services and receive a portion of the wood to sell outright or use to make goods that he would then sell.

By January 1848, most of the work on the mill was completed. One of the last things that needed to be done was widening the tailrace, which is a channel that carries wastewater away from the mill. Widening the tailrace involved blasting though hard rock during most of the day. At night, Marshall diverted water from the American River to the tailrace to use the force of natural water to wash away debris in the channel overnight. He checked on the project every morning and redirected the water back to the river so more blasting could be done during the day.

In the early daylight hours of January 24, 1848, Marshall checked the tailrace. Something caught his eye—something he had never seen before. Mixed in with the silt along the tailrace on that Monday morning, he spotted shiny yellow particles. Some of the particles were of a sandy consistency, but there were some stones as well. In an account of his discovery, Marshall recalled,

> *I was entirely alone at the time. I picked up one or two pieces and examined them attentively; and having some general knowledge of minerals, I could not call to mind more than two which in any way resembled this—sulphuret of iron, very bright and brittle; and gold.* [1]

He then took one of the pea-sized stones, pounded it between two rocks, and noticed that while its shape changed, it did not break. That meant the stone was malleable. An astonished Marshall suddenly realized he was looking at gold.

Frontier Family

The Wimmer family arrived at Sutter's Fort from Missouri in November 1846. Peter and Jennie Wimmer and their seven children were exhausted from the long, difficult trip across the Rocky and Sierra Nevada Mountains to California. They had traveled in a wagon train with 84 other people looking to start a new life in the West. At the fort, the Wimmers worked various jobs for Sutter. When Sutter decided to build a sawmill in 1847, he asked Peter to be Marshall's assistant and Jennie to cook and do laundry for the crew. The Wimmers moved the family to the site of the sawmill where a defining moment in California history awaited them.

Other members of the construction crew were not so quick to proclaim Marshall's find as gold. When he showed his discovery to his workers, many snickered, well aware of other such claims that had turned out to be merely iron pyrite—more commonly known as fool's gold. Jennie Wimmer, the cook at the mill, knew about gold. As a young girl in Auraria, Georgia, she had panned for it. She was the only one at the sawmill who had ever seen a gold nugget. She also knew how to test it.

Marshall gasped as the cook dropped one of the stones he had found in a kettle of lye. "I will throw it into my lye kettle . . .," she declared, ". . . and if it is gold, it will be gold when it comes out."[2] The next morning, Wimmer retrieved the nugget, which was unscathed. The yellow stone passed the test—it was gold. The largest gold rush in US history was about to begin.

John Sutter developed Sutter's Fort and later built the sawmill.

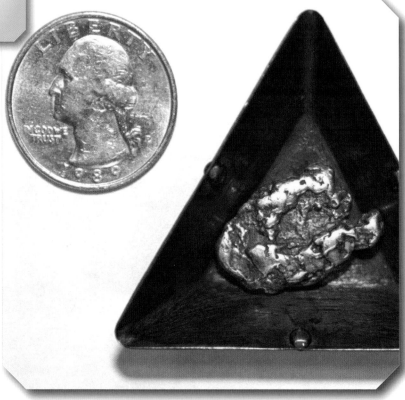

A California gold nugget is displayed
next to a quarter to give an idea of its size.

WORD GETS OUT

our days after Marshall made his discovery,
he took gold samples to New Helvetia
to show Sutter the riches he had drawn from the
American River. Sutter conducted his own test on
the glittering yellow specimens Marshall had brought

with him. He, too, concluded that not only had Marshall found gold, but he had discovered gold of very high quality.

Based on the results of his tests, Sutter declared that the samples of gold found at the sawmill were at least 23 karats. Purity of gold alloy is measured in karats, and 24 karats is the purest.

SILENCE IS GOLDEN

By the time Marshall had brought the gold samples to Sutter, all of the workers at the sawmill were aware that the area was surrounded by gold. Marshall gave his workers permission to search for the precious metal on their off hours. On January 29, 1848, Sutter talked to the sawmill employees. He believed that, for the time being, it was best to keep the gold discovery a secret. He appealed to the workers not to say a word about the unexpected find to anyone.

A Friend in Need

Sutter earned a reputation among pioneers as a very generous man. A pioneer himself, Sutter knew first-hand that frontier life often was unforgiving. Pioneers down on their luck could find free food and shelter at Sutter's Fort for as long as they needed it. Sutter offered jobs to those who wanted to remain in the community, even if it was just for a short time. Those who left the fort and later fell on hard times again were always welcome to return.

Sutter feared for New Helvetia, his economic base. If word leaked out about the gold discovery, little could be done to keep his workers from abandoning their jobs at the fort in an attempt to strike it rich as prospectors. Sutter described what was at stake:

> *Agriculture increased until I had several hundred men working in the harvest fields, and to feed them I had to kill four or sometimes five oxen daily. I could raise 40,000 bushels of wheat without trouble, reap the crops with sickles, thresh it with bones and winnow it in the wind. There were thirty plows running with fresh oxen every morning . . . I had at the time twelve thousand head of cattle, two thousand horses and mules, between ten and fifteen thousand sheep and a thousand hogs. My best days were just before the discovery of gold.*[1]

Sutter worried that his land would be overrun by outsiders in their haste to make their way to gold country. He knew the discovery of gold could enhance the empire he had built, but, far more likely, it could destroy it.

Upheaval in California

At the time Marshall made his discovery, California was going through a turbulent period

A diary entry mentioning the discovery of gold by Marshall

in its history. The United States and Mexico had recently concluded an armed conflict—the Mexican-American War—which lasted from 1846 to 1848.

In 1836, Texas had claimed its independence from Mexico. Texas petitioned for admittance to the United States several times before 1845. The Mexican-American War was touched off when the United States annexed Texas in 1845. Hostilities

broke out on April 25, 1846, when
the first of many border disputes
erupted, and Mexican and US
troops clashed. The fighting spread
to California. The US forces won
numerous battles against Mexico
toward the end of 1847. By 1848, a
full-fledged US victory was at hand.

Technically, Mexico still owned
California when Marshall discovered
gold on January 24, 1848. Nine
days later, however, on February 2,
Mexico signed the Treaty of
Guadalupe Hidalgo, which brought
an end to the war. Under terms
of the treaty, Mexico ceded upper
California to the United States. The
treaty also included present-day
Arizona and New Mexico and parts of
Utah, Nevada, and Colorado. Mexico
relinquished its claims to Texas. The
Rio Grande River was recognized as
the southern border of Texas and
became the boundary between Mexico
and the United States.

Before the Rush

Just prior to the gold rush, many of the US citizens who lived in California were fur trappers, farmers, and cattle or horse ranchers. Mexicans and Native Americans also lived in California at that time. They were united in their love of California's untamed countryside. It was a leisurely place valued for its vast, grassy valleys and majestic mountains with freshwater streams filled with fish. The area was abundant with wild fruits and vegetables—yet to be ravaged by wild-eyed gold seekers.

When the treaty was signed, Mexican officials were completely unaware that gold had been discovered in California. The additional riches yet to be drawn from the area where Marshall had made his discovery were now on land officially controlled by the United States.

A Question of Ownership

As Sutter and Marshall continued to build the sawmill, Sutter worried the US government would not recognize his ownership of the land. Sutter had gained the land when it was under Mexican control. He had even become a Mexican citizen to do so. But when the United States won the Mexican-American War, the land around the mill became public domain. And that was where the gold was.

Before Sutter arrived, the area had been inhabited by Native Americans. The name Coloma meant "beautiful valley" and was derived from the Maidu, a Native American tribe. Sutter had maintained a good relationship with the Maidu, Miwok, Nisenan, and neighboring tribes. In an attempt to establish his rightful ownership of the site, Sutter gathered all the chiefs around the mill in Coloma. He gave them food and clothing in exchange for a three-year lease for the land for the sawmill. But he was well aware that the lease might be worthless. The chiefs who agreed to the lease most likely did not have title to the land.

In hopes of validating the lease, Sutter sent a messenger with a letter and the lease to Colonel Richard B. Mason, the US military governor of California. Sutter hoped to gain his approval and support of the transaction. Mason rejected the lease in spring 1848, saying the US government did not recognize sale or lease documents related to land deals that had been negotiated with Native Americans. Sutter had no rights to the land or the gold it contained. He had no choice but to brace himself for the onslaught of would-be fortune hunters.

A Secret No More

Despite Sutter's pleas for secrecy, news of gold in the American River by Sutter's Mill leaked out. Some of the men had kept Sutter's secret, but most told at least one close relative or friend. The news began to circulate. The first to take action were men working at the fort. As Sutter had dreaded, many abandoned their jobs at the fort and made the trek to Coloma, determined to become rich. "So soon as the secret was out my laborers began to leave me . . . All left, from the clerk to the cook," Sutter reported dejectedly when speaking of the mass exodus.[2]

Others who lived outside the fort were not so easily convinced that gold was scattered throughout the California hills. Those who lived in the small settlement of San Francisco harbored lingering doubts about the gold at Sutter's sawmill. Samuel Brannan, publisher of the *California Star* newspaper, did not

Ulterior Motive?

There may have been reasons for the *California Star*'s downplaying of the discovery of gold at Sutter's sawmill. Brannan had arrived in California in July 1846 and built a commercial empire that ran from San Francisco to Sacramento. He was the publisher of the newspaper, but he was also an entrepreneur. His other ventures included a sawmill, a flour mill, and the general store by Sutter's Fort.

Some believe the paper did not acknowledge the find immediately so Brannan could profit from the discovery. Before returning to San Francisco in May 1848 and proclaiming there was, indeed, gold at Sutter's sawmill in Coloma, he bought every shovel, pick, and bucket in San Francisco. He stocked his store by Sutter's Fort with the items he planned to resell at a hefty markup, once he announced there was gold to be found nearby. In addition, he purchased land in the Coloma area cheaply and built another store and a hotel in preparation of the surge of gold seekers.

Within the first six weeks after Brannan returned to San Francisco and declared gold was at Sutter's Mill in Coloma, he profited greatly. By the end of June, his general store brought in $36,000 ($904,154 in 2010 currency) in profits from miners frantically buying supplies to head to gold country.

give much credence to reports of the discovery and vast amounts of gold contained in the American River. Still, he decided to visit the site in May 1848 to see the gold for himself.

When Brannan returned from Coloma, he was anything but timid about what he had found. The publisher ran through the streets of San Francisco on May 12, waving a bottle of gold dust and yelling, "Gold! Gold! Gold from the American River."[3] Within days, 75 percent of all the men living in San Francisco had left town, bound for gold country. Sailors on whaling ships in the town's harbor abandoned their vessels and headed for Coloma. Men in Monterey, 112 miles (180 km) from San Francisco, soon followed suit. Gold fever was about to spread like wildfire.

Small World

In May 1848, the population of San Francisco was approximately 500. When most of the men left town to find gold in Coloma, San Francisco resembled a ghost town. But that did not last long. The tranquility was broken by thousands of people coming into San Francisco en route to nearby gold country. The migration turned San Francisco from a sleepy port town into a hub of commercial and cultural activity on the West Coast.

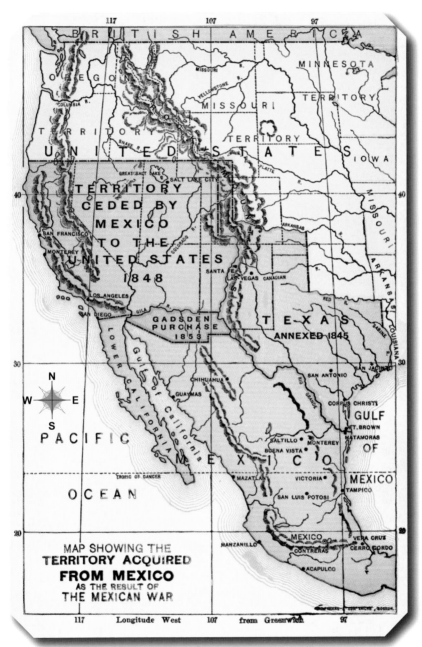

This 1848 map shows the territory the United States acquired from Mexico after the Mexican-American War.

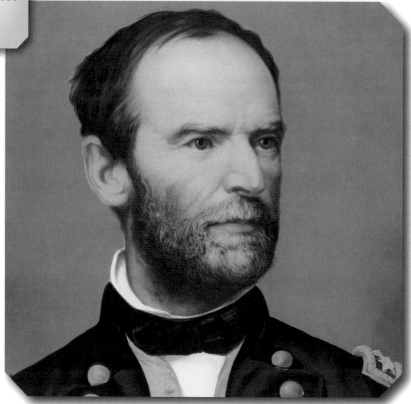

*William Tecumseh Sherman visited the American River
to assess the levels of military desertions due to searches for gold.*

RUSH TO RICHES

By mid-May 1848, an overwhelming number of newspaper reports came out of San Francisco regarding Marshall's gold strike in Coloma. Gold was everywhere—free for the taking. Now, throughout the California countryside, farmers left their fields, business owners shut down their stores, servants walked out on their jobs, and soldiers deserted their posts—all for a chance at once-in-a-lifetime riches hidden in California's Central Valley.

Some men made the trip to gold country by horse, others came on mules, and still others simply loaded their gear into a wheelbarrow and walked. For those going to Coloma from San Francisco, the trip was approximately 140 miles (225 km). Many in the initial wave of gold seekers came to Coloma from points in California much farther away than San Francisco. Distance did not seem to matter.

MASSIVE MILITARY DESERTIONS

Military desertions were of such epic proportions that California's military governor, Colonel Mason, decided to see what the commotion was all about. In June 1848, he visited

Extra Income

Almost everyone who came to gold country saw an opportunity to make money, including Mason, the military governor. Though he found it hard to believe that committed military men would desert their posts to search for gold, he realized it was not easy to make ends meet on a military salary. Shortly after visiting Coloma in June 1848, Mason joined with three partners and opened a store in the area to sell supplies to miners flooding the growing community. He remained in the military while sharing in the store's profits.

Coloma with his adjutant, Lieutenant William Tecumseh Sherman. When Mason arrived, he saw hundreds of men panning and digging for gold at a feverish pace. Men stood in the American River, up to their knees in water, searching for the elusive metal that would make them rich and their dreams come true.

Plenty of white men staked a claim to gold in central California, but Native Americans and Mexicans searched for the precious metal as well. The miners worked alone, but side by side. There was barely an open space without a miner in the section of the American River that flowed through Coloma near the spot where Marshall had made his discovery. Whatever gold these men found was theirs to keep. If a miner left the space where he was working, another gold seeker was free to take that spot.

Mason noted all of this activity. He also gathered some gold in a tea

No Golden Touch

Discovering gold was not a blessing for Marshall. With gold fever in full swing, no men were available to help him run the sawmill he had built, and his venture failed. In 1849, he was forced off the sawmill property by unruly miners in search of gold. Disgusted, he left California soon afterward but returned to Coloma in 1857. In the 1860s, he started a vineyard, but that venture also failed. He then invested in a gold-mining effort in the early 1870s that yielded no return. He died in 1885 and is buried in Coloma.

canister and sent it, together with a report of his findings, to President James K. Polk. His report detailed the staggering amount of gold he saw being drawn from the American River. It would take months before the report and gold samples reached the president.

ALONE OR WITH THE FAMILY

While the early wave of miners were mostly men, it was not long before entire families from California started making their way to the gold fields. It took longer for families to prepare for the trip, which was why most men chose to make the journey alone. Some, however, felt that a family working together would enhance their chances of finding gold and increase the amount of gold they collected. Families abandoned the comfort of their homes and their furnishings for the lure of gold they were not certain they could find.

Traveling by covered wagon, these families would call a tent home during their stay in gold country. At first, women and children helped in the search for gold. But prospecting was such difficult work that the women and young children soon found other ways to earn money while the men—fathers and older sons—searched for gold. Women raised money for the family by cooking meals and doing laundry for miners who simply were too busy working or too tired to cook or do laundry themselves. Children ran errands for the miners or fetched their tools. This helped pay for supplies the family needed during their stay in gold country.

While most of the early gold seekers were people who lived in California, it did not take long for others to migrate to Coloma from points farther away. By August 1848, several thousand

Riches to Rags

Unfortunately, Sutter's worst fears about a gold rush came true. As many as 80,000 miners, including Sutter's employees, joined in the search for gold. With no one left to protect Sutter's Fort, miners and squatters descended on his agricultural community. They took Sutter's crops, killed his cattle, and even settled on his land. Since Mexico had ceded California to the United States, Mexican law was no longer in force, and no US laws were in place to govern the California Territory. Sutter could do nothing to protect his property. In late September 1848, Sutter's eldest son, John Jr., arrived from Switzerland to help his father recoup some of his losses. Now 21 years old, the younger Sutter had not seen his father in 14 years.

John Jr. viewed his father's property as a city of the future and began to lay out plans with Brannan for the city of Sacramento, named after the river. His father was unhappy with the plan because he wanted the city to be named Sutterville. By mid-1849, Sutter sold his fort for $7,000 ($182,840 in 2010 currency) and moved to a farm in the Sacramento valley. He was bankrupt by 1852. Sacramento developed into a major commercial hub during the gold rush years and was eventually selected as the capital of California.

Oregonians, who had heard about the gold in the Central Valley from trappers working their way from California to Oregon Country, had made the trek to Sutter's Mill. They traveled along the Siskiyou Trail, which ran from the Willamette valley in Oregon to California's Central Valley—a direct route to gold country.

In August, newspapers in the eastern United States reported on the gold discovery in California. The first major eastern newspaper to carry the story was the *New York Herald.* On August 19, 1848, the paper ran an eyewitness account from a correspondent who had gone to gold country. New Yorkers were excited by the news of the gold find, but most were not yet ready to commit to a trip out West.

In September, foreign gold seekers arrived in California by ship from Central and South America. They came from Mexico and as far away as Chile and Peru. Native Californians referred to these gold-hungry pioneers who arrived by sea as Argonauts. In Greek mythology, the Argonauts were a band of heroes who sailed on the *Argo* in search of the Golden Fleece. Like the ancient Greek Argonauts, those coming to California by ship made their journey in search of gold.

SUCCESS AND FAILURE

Gold was plentiful in the early days of the gold rush. While some 6,000 people had ventured to California by the end of 1848, that was a minuscule number compared to the tens of thousands who would arrive in 1849. Some prospectors made several thousand dollars a day during the dawn of the gold rush. They needed little more than a pan. But, what was known as "easy gold" was soon gone. A number of prospectors took their newfound wealth and headed home. Others put down roots and started businesses in California.

After a long trip from California, the army courier carrying Mason's report arrived in Washington DC in December 1848. President Polk put some of the gold on display in the library at the US War Department. Newspaper reporters flocked to the display and started running stories about the gold rush with headlines announcing, "Genuine."

While those living in the West were completely caught up in gold fever, it was going to take an extra push to get those in the East to head to California. On December 5, 1848, President Polk gave them that push. In an address to Congress, the president

Gold miners cheering as the supply ship arrives

confirmed the discovery of gold in California's Central Valley:

> *The accounts of the abundance of gold in that territory are of such an extraordinary character as would scarcely*

What Was at Stake

If a miner left a spot where he was working—even for a short time—another miner would jump right in. To provide some order and let other miners know that a spot was taken, gold seekers hammered wooden stakes into the ground around an area where they were working to indicate that the area was spoken for. If there were no stakes in the ground, the space was considered open. When miners left one space for another, they moved the stakes to their new spot.

command belief were they not corroborated by the authentic reports of officers in the public service who visited the mineral district and derived the facts which they detail from personal observation.[1]

Polk's speech prompted gold seekers to migrate to California in numbers never before imagined.

*President James Knox Polk (1845–1849)
announced the discovery of gold to Congress.*

President John Tyler

WESTWARD HO!

The discovery of gold in California brought people from all over the United States westward, but the move west was not a new concept. Vice President John Tyler, an expansionist, became the nation's tenth president (1841–1845) when

President William Henry Harrison died from pneumonia after only one month in office. Tyler favored annexing Texas and signed a joint resolution providing for the annexation of Texas with only three days left in his term. He chose not to run for reelection in 1844. Yet, the issue of expansionism surfaced again. The 1844 election campaign included heavy debate over the country's expansion westward.

DISPUTE OVER EXPANSIONISM

Whig Party candidate Henry Clay was opposed to westward expansion, which included not only Texas but Oregon Country as well. It referred to land in the Pacific Northwest that encompassed what eventually became the Canadian province of British Columbia and the states of Oregon, Washington, Idaho, and parts of Montana and Wyoming. The Democratic presidential nominee,

Presidential Succession

Harrison was elected president in 1840. Upon his death, Tyler was the first vice president to become president upon the death of the incumbent president.

The US Constitution was not clear on the issue of presidential succession. It did not state that the vice president was to take the presidential oath. Many politicians believed the vice president would follow the advice of Harrison's cabinet. Tyler's decision to be sworn in as president set the precedent for a path of succession.

Seven other presidents have died while in office. Zachary Taylor, Warren Harding, and Franklin Delano Roosevelt died from health issues. Abraham Lincoln, James A. Garfield, William McKinley, and John F. Kennedy were assassinated. Still, it was not until 1967 that formalized rules for presidential succession were codified in the Twenty-Fifth Amendment to the US Constitution.

A Man of His Word

Polk said he would serve only one term as president, and he was a man of his word. He did not seek reelection in 1848. Partly due to how much he expanded the nation's borders during his term in office, Polk is considered by historians to have had an enormous impact on the nation.

James K. Polk, favored expansionism, including Mexican-owned California.

In 1845, New Yorker John L. O'Sullivan, editor of the *United States Magazine and Democratic Review*, coined the term *manifest destiny*, which refers to the foundation of the expansionist movement. Manifest destiny was the belief that the United States was destined to expand across North America from the Atlantic Ocean to the Pacific Ocean. Some supporters saw expansionism as a matter of national security. Those who opposed manifest destiny, including Clay, believed it was an immoral plan to seize land that belonged to others.

This expansion would take place despite opposition from Mexico and its claims to Texas, New Mexico, and California. Great Britain also opposed the expansion as it held claims to Oregon Country. Polk won the 1844 election and proceeded with his push westward. The pioneers followed his belief of expansionism.

Westward expansion did not necessarily mean war. In 1845, the United States feared that Great Britain would try to buy California from Mexico. That same year, the United States offered the Mexican government $25 million ($583 million in 2010 currency) for California, but the offer was rejected. Mexico considered the United States a dangerous neighbor. By 1845, there was already tension between Mexico and the United States over the annexation of Texas. Even when Mexico ceded California to the United States after the Mexican-American War ended in 1848, there was a monetary exchange. The United States paid Mexico $15 million ($376.7 million in 2010 currency) for California and additional land that makes up most of the Southwest today.

The dispute with Great Britain over Oregon Country was resolved by both governments through a peaceful treaty in 1846. The Oregon Treaty set the northern limit for annexation of Oregon Country by the United States at the forty-ninth parallel. This is the US border between present-day British Columbia east to Manitoba on the Canadian side and from the state of Washington to Minnesota on the US side.

Read All about It

The May 17, 1848, issue of the *Californian* newspaper commented on the speed of men leaving San Francisco for gold country. It referred to the mania as *gold fever*. This was the first time the term was used to describe the behavior of masses of people who were sparked by the passion for gold.

The long, difficult overland trip to the West made migration slow at first. But the lure of gold drove people to California from all parts of the United States. Gold seekers arrived from China, Chile, Mexico, and even the Hawaiian Islands. The population in the United States began to shift once gold was discovered in California's Central Valley in 1848. Though unexpected, the discovery of gold in California meshed with Polk's passion for westward expansion. Population growth in the West was also propelled by immigrants from Europe, Asia, and South America who came to start a new life in the Western Hemisphere by scooping up gold in California.

Newspapers Spread the Word

Accelerating the move to California during the gold rush were glowing stories of quick riches and easy opportunities in the West carried in newspapers all over the country. At first, newspaper editors in San Francisco did not know what to make of the gold discovery in Coloma. The *Californian* finally ran a small article about the discovery on March 15, 1848, nearly two months after Marshall's historic discovery. Once *California Star* publisher Brannan went to

Coloma and saw the gold, newspapers in the West jumped all over the story. Newspapers in the East did not start running stories until late August 1848.

In the mid-1800s, newspapers relied on other newspapers to get their stories. One newspaper would rewrite an article published in another paper, embellishing the tale in the process. While many of the stories about the gold rush were based on fact, some incorporated myths to spice up the information. As people from the Midwest and

Progressive Thinking

Women arriving in California found that the area was much more forward thinking when it came to a woman's property rights than the East. When California drew up a constitution in 1849, it was based on the Spanish and French legal systems and accorded greater rights to women than the British legal system that was used as the model in the eastern United States. Under the California Constitution,

All property, both real and personal, of the wife, owned or claimed by her before marriage, and that acquired afterwards by gift, devise or descent, shall be her separate property.[1]

In the East, by contrast, a woman's property became her husband's upon marriage, and she lost all her property rights unless she was widowed.

At the California Constitutional Convention on September 1, 1849, one delegate cautioned against giving women separate property rights. He claimed it would promote divorce. Delegates who grew up in the West felt that giving women separate property rights would encourage females to settle in California. By adopting the constitutional provision guaranteeing married women's property rights, California became one of the more progressive states in the nation when it was admitted to the Union on September 9, 1850.

the East started moving to gold country, newspapers began printing firsthand accounts of the gold rush sent to them by volunteer correspondents. Most of these correspondents were gold seekers themselves.

Mail was slow, so the accounts could be months old by the time they were published. Nevertheless, people who could not make the trek to gold country were captivated by the accounts, and newspapers printed all the information about the gold rush they could get. Some prospectors kept diaries of their travels to California and what they found once they reached gold country. They often sent their diaries back home, and newspapers printed entries on an ongoing basis. Some of the articles developed quite a following as they described the joys and hardships of the long journey to California's Central Valley. Newspapers across the country were plentiful and most had at least one person from their local area willing to keep hometown readers transfixed by gold-hunting stories. From 1849 to well into the gold rush years, newspapers in the East carried ads for sea voyages to California and all the equipment anyone could ever need to mine gold.

Newspaper columns cited the best western routes and carried stories about the latest inventions

A California gold rush mining camp

that made mining easier. Most of the inventions, however, did not work and were never meant to. They were nothing more than get-rich-quick schemes devised by those trying to persuade gold-seeking hopefuls to part with their new fortune before they even made it. *New York Tribune* editor Horace Greeley wrote in his column, "The only machinery necessary in the new Gold mines of California is a stout pair of arms, a shovel, and a tin pan."[2]

Miners by the Numbers

By the end of 1848, approximately 5,000 gold seekers had made their way to the gold fields in California's Central Valley. By the end of 1849, more than 90,000 gold seekers had ventured there. The total reached 300,000 in 1854. More than half of the gold seekers were in their twenties. Nine out of ten were men. The influx was a boom to businesses in towns such as San Francisco and Sacramento. In the gold rush, a town that experienced fast economic growth became known as a boomtown.

Newspapers became popular in mining towns. In mining towns where no printing presses were available, news was handwritten. Getting information out about the latest happenings—including new gold finds, social events, and supply deliveries—was vital. News catering to particular ethnic groups was written in Chinese, Spanish, German, French, and other languages.

While thousands made their way to California in 1848, tens of thousands followed in 1849. They came by land and by sea, but few were prepared for what they would experience along the way and once they reached California. ⌒

New York Tribune *editor Horace Greeley*

A Currier & Ives lithograph depicts inventive ways to reach California.

PERILS AT SEA

*I*n the late 1840s, migration to California
was difficult. To make a trip to gold
country, especially from the eastern United States or
the Midwest, required commitment and planning.
The trip could take six months over land by horse-

drawn covered wagon. There were no cross-country trains. The journey was even longer by sea. Despite the hardships, gold-hungry people swarmed to California in 1849. Native Californians called the new arrivals the forty-niners.

THE PULL WESTWARD

Incentives other than the possibility of finding gold drew people to the West as well. Land was cheap for those who settled on it. There was little free land and many cities were crowded east of the Mississippi River. It was much less crowded in the West than in the East, and life was less restrained. Since most of the men already living in California had left their jobs in search of gold, there was a shortage of workers. In order to lure people to take jobs in the West, employers on the West Coast offered higher wages than those in the East.

Investors

Many easterners who felt they were too old to survive a trip to the West Coast invested in gold expeditions. They financed a trip to gold country by younger, stronger men. In return, the investors would get their money back and share in the profits once gold was struck. Formal agreements were drawn up to spell out the terms of the arrangement.

Slavery was still legal in parts of the United States—primarily in the South. Some slaves were brought to California by their owners to work the mines. But California planned to enter the Union as a free state, where slavery was banned. This decision was made to help the mining economy, but it did not end racism.

Easterners who decided to venture westward usually made the trip by sea. The voyage was lengthy—approximately 17,000 miles (27,359 km)—and took five to eight months. It some cases, it could take as long as a year. Prices for the ocean voyage ranged from $100 to $300 (approximately $2,612 to $7,836 in 2010 currency). Ships traveled south along the East Coast of the United States and around Cape Horn, which is the southernmost point in South America, and north to San Francisco. The ships were usually overbooked. Food went stale or rancid en route. The lack of fresh fruits and vegetables caused many to contract scurvy, a disease brought on by lack of vitamin C. The supply of drinking water routinely ran low, and seasickness and cholera outbreaks were common.

Shipwrecks and other disasters at sea threatened travelers. Fierce storms battered ships as they

Sea routes to California

rounded Cape Horn. Some people were tossed overboard, and the sea was too rough to save them. In 1849, more than 500 ships made the trip. Those who made it to San Francisco arrived exhausted. Yet they still had to trek 140 miles (225 km) by land to reach gold country.

In Search of a Quicker Route

Impatient gold seekers tried to find a faster sea route to San Francisco—and they did. But that shortcut involved even greater risk. Voyagers first took a steamship from the East Coast of the United

States to Panama in Central America. On the next portion of the trip, they crossed the Isthmus of Panama, which links North and South America by a narrow strip of land from the Caribbean Sea to the Pacific Ocean. Travelers crossed the isthmus by taking a canoe up the Chagres River in central Panama for the first 75 miles (121 km) and made the final 25 miles (40 km) by mule. When the crossing was completed, they boarded another ship bound for San Francisco. If nothing went awry, this route took about two months. This

The Need for Speed

Rufus Porter, the founder of *Scientific American*, devised a better way to get people to California. Porter drew up plans for an 800-foot (244-m) propeller-driven balloon airship, similar to today's blimps. The airship, which was to be powered by steam engines, was designed to carry 50 to 100 people at a time and travel at 50 miles per hour (80 km/h). Porter advertised this new form of transportation in newspapers as a way to get to gold country in only three days, and 200 people signed up for the trip. Each paid a deposit of $50 ($1,306 in 2010 currency) on the fare of $200 ($5,224 in 2010 currency). Technical difficulties plagued the project, however, and it was finally abandoned in 1854.

In 1853, William Thomas, an entrepreneur and inventor, came up with the idea of a wind wagon. His concept combined the bottom of a covered wagon with the sail of a sailboat. Thomas believed high winds in the West would blow the prairie schooner across the Great Plains at 15 miles per hour (24 km/h), which would get people to California faster than a horse-drawn wagon. It was designed to carry people and goods. Thomas had financial backers, but after his first prototype crashed, many of those backers pulled out, and the idea was abandoned.

route saved time but was much more costly at $400 to $600 per person (approximately $10,448 to $15,672 in 2010 currency) than the voyage around Cape Horn.

There were several downsides to this route, however. Besides incurring the extra cost for transportation across the isthmus and lodging there, many came down with tropical diseases, such as malaria and yellow fever, while traveling through Panama. Crossing the Central American rain forest, a steamy, swampy jungle with thick underbrush, was difficult. Voyagers faced many hardships, from treacherous mud and dangerous reptiles to disease-carrying mosquitoes. Travelers were warned to pack sparingly, but often their personal belongings proved to be too heavy when crossing the isthmus. Much of the luggage was abandoned along the route.

Biggest Risk

The most deadly of all challenges during the gold rush was cholera, an infection of the small intestine. Cholera spread easily, especially when sanitary conditions were poor, as they were on ships, along overland trails, and in mining camps. The disease racked the body with high fevers, diarrhea, vomiting, and dehydration. Common remedies prescribed by doctors at the time had no impact. Cholera killed quickly, often within a day of the appearance of symptoms.

Those who survived the journey were often stranded when they reached the Pacific because ships were not regularly scheduled to make the final leg of the journey. Ships to take travelers from Panama to San Francisco arrived infrequently, and travelers often waited weeks in disease-infested coastal towns for a ship to pull into port. During their stopover, they crammed into small bamboo huts to avoid getting soaked by the tropical rains. The travelers were not accustomed to the Panamanian menu of grilled iguana and baked monkey that was common during their stay. Once a ship arrived, it was besieged by eager gold seekers desperate to reach gold country.

Some blacks chose to sail the Panamanian route to riches. While this trip was shorter, they had the additional worry of coming across Panamanian slave traders, who would try to kidnap them and force them into a life of slavery.

San Francisco: A Rude Welcome to the West

San Francisco was once the site of a Spanish missionary established in the eighteenth century. When weary travelers reached San Francisco, they found a town on the brink of becoming a major

city, but one that was ill-prepared
for new arrivals. As there were no
docks, the passengers slogged through
deep mud to get to shore. Once they
reached dry land, worn-out travelers
found that there was not enough
housing to handle the onslaught of
fortune hunters. People desperate
for housing sought out some of the
ships sailors had abandoned when
they took off for the gold fields. The
travelers turned these empty vessels
into makeshift hotels as a place to rest
for a few days.

At first glance, San Francisco was
a disappointment for many. The city
had no place to store baggage. Food
was in short supply and expensive.
The city, still in its infancy, was dirty
and loud. Jennie Megquier took the
short route to California through
Panama with her husband, Thomas,
in the winter of 1849. After enduring
the strenuous trip, Jennie summed
up her feelings about San Francisco

Few Rules

The gold rush started
as California was going
through a period of tran-
sition. None of the towns
in the new US territory of
California had local gov-
ernments, so gold seekers
entered a world where
few rules applied. Small
mining towns made their
own rules, which varied
from town to town. On
the upside, there was no
government tax on any of
the gold gathered by the
miners.

by saying, "It is the most God-forsaken country in the world."[1]

Though the voyage by sea was difficult, the westward trip over land was more arduous. Many who took the overland route knew little or nothing about surviving in the outdoors and lacked the skills vital to surviving the demanding journey. ⌐

Miners working in a river valley

Stagecoaches brought gold seekers to California.

A Long, Unforgiving Trail

*O*f the 90,000 gold seekers who came to California in 1849, approximately half came by sea and half traveled over land. Most of those who made the overland journey to fill their pockets with gold were from the Midwest.

The starting points for the trips to California were usually Saint Joseph or Independence, Missouri. Gold seekers from eastern states who could not afford to make the trip to California by sea took the overland route by covered wagon or on horseback. Those from New York City who wanted to stake their claim to gold in California had to travel to Missouri, which was quite a trip in itself. It included taking a passenger ship from New York to Baltimore, a train to Cumberland, Maryland, and a stagecoach over the Allegheny Mountains to the Monongahela River where a steamship ran to Pittsburgh. From Pittsburgh, another steamship ran down the Ohio River to the Mississippi River. When it stopped in Saint Louis, it was easy to find another steamship to Saint Joseph or Independence. From there, it was another 2,100 miles (3,380 km) to California. Though many thought an

Plenty of Pull

Many forty-niners chose oxen, rather than horses, to pull their wagons. Oxen were much stronger than horses and could go longer without water. However, they were slower than horses and mules. Mules were also used to pull covered wagons westward during the gold rush. Mules provided added security at night because they started braying when a stranger entered the camp.

Mississippi steamer near Saint Louis

overland trip to California would be less expensive
than the voyage by sea, the overland trip could cost as
much as $700 ($18,284 in 2010 currency).

Timing Was Crucial

The overland trip was a seasonal event. It made no
sense to attempt it in winter. Word reached people
too late in 1848 to start the trip westward and avoid
winter conditions. By mid-April 1849, forty-niners
began gathering in Missouri in anticipation of the
journey west. The trip began in early May when

there was enough grass on the prairie for the horses, mules, and oxen pulling the wagons to graze on. The wagon trains had to reach San Francisco by early October or risk being trapped in the mountains by an early snowstorm. At best, a covered wagon traveled 16 miles (26 km) a day—usually less. It covered less ground when the trails became muddy. Some who traveled light planned to ride on horseback.

Before leaving Missouri, people organized themselves into traveling companies. They chose a leader and drafted a set of rules that each member of the company had to abide by. It was important to have people with different talents in the groups. Blacksmiths, carpenters, farmers, tailors, bakers, doctors, and artisans all brought useful talents.

Most packed their belongings in a wooden wagon. The canvas cover was waterproofed with linseed oil. Some families had to use more than one wagon. Each family had to pack enough food and water to last six months—it was uncertain if there would be anywhere along the trail to get supplies.

One of the most important jobs was learning how to work with the team of animals pulling the covered wagon. Joseph Goldsborough Bruff, the captain of a wagon train of Washington DC forty-niners, watched a group of easterners who had just arrived in Missouri and tried to train a team of mules. He observed, "Most of them knew as much about mules when they arrived here, as the mules did about them."[1]

Wagon trains left at planned intervals to avoid backups along the trail. But at the height of the traveling season, wagons stretched throughout the trail. "In every direction, as far as can be seen, the country is speckled with the white tents and wagons of the emigrants," Bruff wrote in his journal.[2] He also made sketches of the landscape.

Safety in Numbers

Even before the migration to California began in earnest, news circulated about how demanding it was to make the lengthy trip. The majority of men who wanted to seek their fortunes in the California gold fields formed travel associations. These groups were made up of as few as five men and often more. Each man contributed an equal amount of money to pay for supplies and travel expenses. In return, the men shared equally in any profits the expedition reaped. The association provided its members with a sense of security during the trip and once they were in gold country.

Individuals and families had no knowledge about what the trip entailed. Organizers of these associations determined what was needed—both for the trip and once the gold seekers arrived—and prepared for any situations that might arise.

These groups had informal, but very detailed, articles of association, specifying a means of self-government and the rules of conduct for the membership. The associations were usually made up of like-minded people, such as people who agreed not to travel on the Sunday Sabbath or people who refused to engage in gambling. This made for a less stressful journey.

The Treacherous California Trail

The most popular overland route, the California Trail, ran from Missouri to California. Wagon trains took various trails to the Humboldt River valley in Nevada. The first part of the trip was relatively easy.

However, city dwellers had a difficult time adjusting to the rugged trail life. Hauling water, cooking over an open fire, tending to animals, pushing wagons stuck in mud, and collecting buffalo chips (dried manure) for the fire were new to them. Many were shaken by the sounds of the wilderness— wolves howling, panthers screeching.

Travelers endured unfamiliar discomforts and inconveniences. These included dry, irritated, sun-baked skin, day after sweaty day without a bath, and wearing the same dirty, dusty clothes for weeks. Personal hygiene was minimal or nonexistent; many of the pioneers had an odor. Some friendly Native Americans who came in contact with the wagon trains along the trail thought the gold seekers were uncivilized because they failed to clean themselves.

Approximately half of the livestock and one-third of the covered wagons that started the overland journey from Missouri to California completed the trip. Many wagons broke down, could not be

repaired, and were left on the trail.
Disease wiped out entire families
as well as the animals pulling the
wagons. Overburdened wagon trains
usually had to leave the wagons and
the property of the deceased families
at the site where the last family
member died.

The toughest part of the trip lay
beyond the valley—crossing the Forty-
Mile Desert. This stretch of land had
no drinkable water. The animals and
people struggled through choking,
blinding sand and scorching heat.
The deep sand hindered the wagon
wheels as well as the horses, oxen, and
mules. Wagons that became stuck in
the sand needed lighter loads, which
meant leaving some belongings.
Everything except absolute necessities
was left behind. The desert was
littered with people's belongings and
the bodies of animals that perished.
The stench was often overwhelming.
Once travelers conquered the

Water Shortage

Some travelers failed to bring enough water to cross the Forty-Mile Desert. This led some California entrepreneurs to head to the desert with barrels of water. They sold the water by the glass. Prices for one glass of water ranged from $1 to $100 ($26.12 to $2,612 in 2010 currency), depending on the demand. Steep prices aside, there were always plenty of takers.

desert, they faced crossing the rugged Sierra Nevada Mountains. Early snowfalls could make the last leg of the trip deadly. Still, they pushed forward. They knew that on the other side of those mountains the California gold fields awaited.

Dangers en Route

As gold seekers left the more settled part of the country, they were understandably concerned about the dangers that lay ahead. Some feared attacks by hostile Native Americans. However, most of those fears stemmed from rumors pioneers heard before leaving Missouri. While some attacks did occur, there were greater dangers to worry about. Many more people traveling westward died from diseases—such as Rocky Mountain spotted fever, cholera, and dysentery—and accidents than attacks by renegade Native Americans.

Little or no medicine was available on the trail. Disease spread quickly through the wagon trains, especially among children. Deaths from disease occurred frequently. People drowned as wagons crossed swollen rivers. Quicksand was always a threat. Some children fell out of wagons and were crushed underneath the wheels. Men who had never carried

Though Californians were preoccupied with the gold rush and visions of quick riches, small groups of nameless and brave individuals heard of wagon train stragglers left behind on the trail and set out to rescue them. Experienced on the frontier, these rescuers packed rations and supplies and headed out to the trail to find those left behind and bring them to safety.

John Sutter sent expeditions to help stranded travelers. These included the 1847 Donner-Reed group of 20 wagons and 90 people. Following a route suggested in The Emigrants Guide to Oregon and California by Lansford Hastings, the group was stranded in the Sierra Nevada Mountains. Rescue parties from Sutter's Fort rescued 48 of the travelers.

These rescuers did this out of compassion and asked for no money in return. Had it not been for their selfless efforts, hundreds more would have perished en route to gold country.

a gun accidentally shot each other or themselves. It was not uncommon for children to be orphaned during these trips and taken in by another family. Families who lost loved ones along the trail had to bury them quickly.

When the hardships became too tough to handle, some people went back home. This decision had to be made before the wagon trains started crossing the Rocky Mountains. At that point, retracing steps was more dangerous than moving forward. Despite it all, most kept going as visions of gold drove them onward. The journey, however, was life changing. No one who survived was ever the same.

Covered wagons crossed the Sierra Nevada Mountains
to reach California.

Chinese immigrants joined in the search for gold and riches.

CULTURE OF HATRED

old seekers also came by ship from as far away as Europe and China. For these immigrants, gold was only one reason to make the trip to California. Many of the immigrants' home countries were experiencing conflicts, famine, and high unemployment. This prompted them to travel halfway around the world to forge a new life in a place where the riches seemed easy and endless.

Unrest in France, Germany, and other parts of Europe in 1848 prompted many Europeans to flee social and political oppression. Many chose California to try their hand at prospecting. News of gold in California reached France in November 1848, and the first full ship of French gold seekers left for San Francisco in January 1849. Other ships soon followed. Those who wanted to escape the Great Famine in Ireland (1845–1849), also known as the Potato Famine, took a chance on moving to San Francisco and trying to strike gold as well.

Thousands of Chinese immigrants came to the California gold fields to escape poverty, food shortages, and joblessness in their native land. Despite articles in London newspapers denouncing gold rush reports as "Yankee humbug," even British gold seekers descended on California.[1] The *Liverpool Mail* newspaper wrote of the gold rush, "The people that believe these things are only fools."[2] These foreign forty-niners joined fortune hunters from America in the gold fields that the miners called the diggings.

Welcome Turns to Resentment

At first, new arrivals at the gold fields were received warmly. As the onslaught continued, however, miners who had been in gold country since 1848 began to resent the newcomers. Early reports from California's Central Valley were true: Gold, indeed, was everywhere. But that did not last long. Easy-to-find gold was quickly picked clean. Then, the real work started. Those who arrived after late 1849 found miners putting in long days of hard labor without hitting pay dirt.

In 1850, author and journalist John David Borthwick traveled from New York City to the diggings in California. Like many others who joined the gold rush late, he was disappointed when he got there. He wrote, "Men used to pick chunks of gold out of crevices . . . with no other tool than a bowie knife, but those days are gone."[3] Many of the forty-niners who made the seemingly endless trip to California discovered only one sure thing: prospecting was very hard work.

Discrimination and Intimidation

When gold became harder to find, someone had to be at fault. Impatient, discouraged, and desperate,

Prospectors wash gravel, looking for gold.

Anglo miners targeted minorities and foreigners as the ones to blame. They accused people of other colors or nationalities, whom they once worked with side by side, of stealing from them. White miners accused Native Americans of taking land that was never theirs.

As miners spread out in California's Central Valley in search of gold, they had little regard for people living on the land they wanted. Greed had overtaken them and nothing stood in the way of their self-interests. Native Americans were routinely thrown off their own land. Miners did not hesitate to kill Native Americans who refused to leave. In most cases, miners had far better weapons than the Native Americans.

Legislative Discrimination

Discrimination during the gold rush came in the form of legislation. The California State Legislature passed the Foreign Miners Tax on April 13, 1850. Under the law, all miners who were not US citizens had to pay a monthly fee of $20 (approximately $522 in 2010 currency) to mine for gold in California. That amounted to approximately one ounce (28.3 g) of gold—a hefty sum. At the time, California was not yet a US state. Since it was a territory, the US Congress could have repealed the law, but it did nothing.

The law applied only to foreigners. The French, Mexican, and Peruvian miners protested. On May 19, 1850, miners organized a rebellion of as many as 4,000 miners against the tax in the gold-mining town of Sonora. The miners ran onto the streets shouting revolutionary slogans. The next day, hundreds of American miners stormed the town and arrested the rebellion's organizers. The unrest worsened and, greatly outnumbered, the troops left. The legislature agreed to reconsider the tax. But in the time it took to repeal it, 80 percent of the foreign miners had left California rather than pay the tax. Those departures hurt merchants, who had fewer customers to buy their goods. The law was repealed on March 14, 1851.

White miners burned down entire Native American villages to seize the land they wanted for mining purposes. These miners, ruthless in their actions, were never charged with any crime.

When California became a state in 1850, elected officials opposed giving Native Americans land rights or legal rights. The state's congressional delegation fought any attempts by the US government to forge fair treaties with Native Americans and give them land grants.

Peter H. Burnett, California's first elected governor, said in his annual message in 1851,

> *That a war of extermination will continue to be waged between the races, until the Indian race becomes extinct, must be expected. While we cannot anticipate this result but with painful regret, the inevitable destiny of the race is beyond the power or wisdom of man to avert.*[4]

His remarks inflamed an already difficult situation. He and the

No Immunity

In 1845, approximately 150,000 Native Americans lived in California. By 1870, only 30,000 remained in the state. Though many Native Americans died violently at the hands of white gold miners, many more died of diseases. Cholera and Rocky Mountain spotted fever, to which Native Americans had no immunity, were brought to gold country by white American and European miners. Native Americans also died of starvation as miners destroyed food supplies by ravaging Native American farmlands, hunting grounds, and streams that contained fish.

California State Legislature simply
did not care.

Targeting Foreigners and Blacks

Discrimination, however, did not
end with Native Americans. Mexicans
were also targeted. Many miners
fought in the Mexican-American
War and still carried a grudge against
the Mexicans. Under the Treaty of
Guadalupe Hidalgo, the United
States agreed to recognize the land
rights of Mexican citizens who still
lived in California after the war.
This included John Sutter, who
had become a Mexican citizen years
earlier to establish a land claim in
California. But white miners forcibly
took over the Mexicans' land, paid
nothing for it, and harassed the
Mexicans until they left. Once again,
the US government did nothing to
stop this.

Not about Freedom

After compromises in Congress in 1850 to balance the slave and free states, California joined the Union as a free state. California proved valuable to the Union during the Civil War (1861–1865). Its gold helped to pay for much of the war effort. But California's antislavery stand had less to do with civil rights than economics. Californians believed there was no way to compete in the gold fields with those who used slave labor to mine.

The hatred spread to Chilean miners. Chilean miners came to California gold country with experience mining in their native land. As a result, they had great success in California and white miners wanted them to leave. Gangs of white miners used intimidation and violence to strong-arm these miners into fleeing California.

Black miners, some of whom were slaves, initially mined alongside everyone else. That changed when all blacks were told by mobs of white miners to abandon their claims or face death. No action was taken against these intimidators, and no arrests were made.

Perhaps no group was shown more contempt and suffered greater discrimination than the Chinese miners. They had a strong work ethic and were willing to work hard, often in areas others had given up on. Many Americans resented those who

A New Tax

On May 4, 1852, the California State Legislature passed a new Foreign Miners Tax. This targeted any foreign miner who did not become a US citizen. Chinese miners were prime targets of this tax. At the time, Chinese were ineligible to become US citizens under federal law. This tax was three dollars a month ($78 in 2010 currency), a large sum, considering that most Chinese miners only made approximately six dollars ($157 in 2010 currency) a month. Some Chinese miners ran and hid when tax collectors came, but most paid. The tax was effective until 1870.

clearly differed in appearance and cultural practices. The determination on the part of the Chinese miners frequently turned these sites, once thought to be worthless, into gold-producing land. That success enraged white miners, who lashed out at these men by violently attacking and robbing them.

Many victimized by prejudice and discrimination left gold country, but plenty stayed on and were determined to fight back even if no one supported them. In response, many white merchants gave minorities and foreigners less in exchange for their gold than they gave white miners. In turn, minorities and foreigners opened their own businesses and served those who were treated unfairly elsewhere. Once established, these businesses contributed to California's development into a prosperous state. As minority and foreign business owners gained wealth, they acquired a voice in California and began to fight for their rights. But no voices were raised to champion what may have suffered the most during the gold rush—the California environment.

Prospectors panning for gold

Prospectors used a device called a rocker or cradle to separate the pebbles from the gold nuggets.

SINS OF GOLD COUNTRY

*P*anning for gold was not a cost-effective method, even though all that was needed was a shallow pan resembling a pie tin. Miners stood in the American River and dipped the pan in the water. Once water was in the pan, the miners swirled the water around. The heavier gold ended up in the bottom of the pan, while the lighter sand and water spilled out over the rim.

The process seemed easy, but it took hours of standing in the river, often in frigid water, and bending repeatedly to scoop up water. Days of work often yielded little return. As a result of the backbreaking labor involved in panning and working in a wet environment, many miners suffered from rheumatism. Those who experienced rheumatism, a painful disorder of stiffness and swollen joints, were usually forced to give up their search for gold.

Soon, the pan and other early hand tools used at the dawn of the gold rush were replaced with newer mining technology. The rocker, or cradle, was first used on March 9, 1848. More sand and gravel could be processed in a day by using a rocker than the old-fashioned panning method. As the device was rocked back and forth, water washed away the sand and gravel, leaving the heavier gold behind. The rocker took more than one man to operate. The new technology forced miners to work in teams or small companies and share the profits. The rockers were expensive at an average cost of $100 ($2,612 in 2010 currency).

Environmental Devastation

Giving no thought to how they damaged the pristine California landscape, miners diverted streams and dammed rivers to expose the soil lying in the beds beneath the waterways that was rich with gold. This flooded farmlands, ruining prime agricultural terrain. Once the riverbed or streambed was exposed, the miners dug up the rich soil, separated the gold, and kept the precious metal. They left a flooded, excavated, devastated countryside behind.

When gold was found, it fed the miners' insatiable greed for more. When picks and shovels did not dig up the ground fast enough, miners started dredging. They used large buckets to scoop up huge amounts of earth, which gouged deep into riverbeds and riverbanks. As the gold rush continued, more sophisticated machines were used for dredging. These contained more buckets that displaced even more earth. Once the gold was separated from the soil, the excess gravel, rock silt, and mud were piled on the riverbanks. Some piles reached as high as a seven-story building and dwarfed the rivers in the Sacramento valley. These barren hills still remain today, a sore legacy of the environmental evils of the gold rush.

Miners knew the gold they found in rivers and streams had come from another source. They started searching for the mother lode, which was usually found in rock. In 1852, mining companies formed. Many people who had staked their own claims found they needed to work for these companies to make ends meet. The mining companies used hydraulic mining to break through the rock— one of the most environmentally destructive mining techniques ever invented. Miners sprayed powerful

Powerful Idea

The first person to use hydraulic mining was Anthony Chabot, a gold rush pioneer who hailed from Quebec, Canada. In 1852, he constructed the first hose used to cut through the tough California mountainside. In 1853, he joined with Eli Miller and Edward Matteson to build a better hose. Miller, a tinsmith, came up with the idea of adding a nozzle. The hoses and nozzles were improved at a rapid pace as hydraulic mining continued to be refined.

Companies that funded hydraulic and hard-rock mountain mining extracted more gold. It was much faster than panning. These mining techniques required large workforces and huge amounts of capital for equipment and supplies. Only large mining companies could afford to use these techniques.

By the mid-1850s, companies had put the individual miner out of business. Still, these operations did create many jobs for men in California's Central Valley. Miners worked for the companies on a salary basis. The days of a miner panning for his own gold and keeping whatever he found were gone.

However, in 1882, a lawsuit was brought against the mines for dumping the debris of hydraulic mining into the rivers. In 1883, Judge Lorenzo Sawyer ruled against the hydraulic mining companies. Hydraulic mining was no longer allowed in California.

streams of water through canvas hoses with tapered nozzles. The water sliced into clay, gravel, and rocks, ripping away entire mountainsides to expose the gold. This violently reconfigured the topography and reduced the landscape to slush. The slush was washed through a sluice—a water-channeled, gold-washing device—to isolate the gold.

But some gold always slipped away. In an attempt to limit that loss, miners poured mercury into the sluice to form an amalgam of gold and mercury. The gold was then extracted from the amalgam by heating up the compound. However, a great deal of the mercury—as much as 7,600 short tons (6,895 metric tons)—washed downstream and made its way into the environment. Mercury, also known as quicksilver, is toxic to the environment and to humans. Mercury levels continue to remain high in some parts of California due to its use in mining.

Liquid Assets

Water was one of the elements necessary to keep gold-mining operations running. Supplying water to gold-mining companies became a very profitable business. Water companies concentrated on getting the valued resource from streams in the Sierra Nevada Mountains to mining locations. To do this, they built long channels. Building water channels required investment capital, but the need for water was so great that water companies could charge high prices for their product. Investment capital was quickly recouped.

With the gold removed, the rest of the mountainside was considered nothing more than mining debris. The debris slid into the Central Valley, decimating streams, rivers, and thousands of acres of rich farmland, killing fish and wildlife in the process. Entire towns were covered by 25 feet (7.6 m) of mud and rock. When miners destroyed one mountain, they moved on to the next, caring nothing about the land they had demolished.

Hydraulic mining uprooted and overran lush forests, brutalized acres of woodland, and caused economic misery for the logging industry. It flooded the Central Valley and destabilized slopes, ridge tops, and hillsides in gold country. Farmers watched as their land was buried—along with part of the future of California agriculture. Farmers fought the hydraulic miners in court until a judge restricted the practice of hydraulic mining in the mid-1880s. But, by then, severe damage had been done.

Eventually, hard-rock mining took center stage. Once again, this was a technique that required financial backing and specialized skills. Hard-rock mining required tunneling through thousands of miles of mountains to reach gold encased in veins. While this type of mining caused flooding, cave-ins,

Mining for gold in a tunnel was expensive and dangerous.

and irreversible damage to the mountainside, it continued unabated until the 1940s. Today, California still grapples with the environmental aftermath of the gold rush. Some rivers, lakes, and streams will never be restored; prime agricultural soil has been lost forever.

CRIME WAVES

Other social ills cast a pall over the gold rush as well. The biggest was crime. Some men did not come to the gold fields to mine—they came to rob miners. Thieves often entered mining towns at night and robbed miners while they slept. More brazen robbers held a six-shooter to a miner's face and took what they wanted. At the height of the gold rush, the town of Marysville had 17 murders in one week. In early gold rush days, there were no police officers in California's Central Valley. Even San Francisco did not have a police department. Lawlessness held gold country in an iron grip. Protection came down to groups of vigilantes who took justice into their own hands. In January 1849, three men who had been caught stealing money in El Dorado County were lynched. This was the first lynching of the gold rush.

Because of the absence of laws governing California, many mining towns set up their own legal system with their rules for handling criminals. Vigilante justice was crude and often based more on rumor than fact. Yet, it filled a void, and many mining towns felt it was the only way to provide security or any kind of law and order. Hundreds of thousands of dollars' worth of gold was in some of these mining towns, and robbers and murderers would stop at nothing to seize it. This was their way of getting rich during the gold rush. Volunteers served on vigilance committees. Members, few with

Taking a Gamble

Gambling halls were lucrative businesses. The owners of these establishments in San Francisco acknowledged that they were running a business to get as much of the miners' gold as possible. The miners often lost every cent they had made mining.

Gambling was legal in most parts of the United States. In gold country, gambling began as the only form of entertainment. Professional gamblers soon swarmed into San Francisco to "unburden" miners of their gold. Professional gamblers were tolerated in most places. Cheaters were not, and they were shot. Some form of gambling took place in most gold-mining towns. But in San Francisco, it was an event paired with music, dancing, and beverages. A Methodist missionary who witnessed the activity in a gold rush gambling hall commented, "The utter recklessness, the perfect 'Abandon' with which they drink, gamble, and swear is altogether astounding."[1]

any legal training, fulfilled the roles of judge, jury, and, if necessary, executioner. Oftentimes, the wrong person was accused and punished for a crime.

One mining town became known as Hangtown. The miners were quick to enforce laws against anyone suspected of committing a crime. Following what the community felt was a fair hearing, the most violent offenders were hanged. The tree used for the hangings became a tourist attraction. In 1854, residents felt the town's name did not reflect positively on the town and the name was changed to Placerville. Still, the town's reputation achieved the desired effect and crime was reduced substantially.

Hydraulic mining was profitable for the mining companies but damaged the environment.

*These gold bars were recovered from the Central America steamship.
In 1857, on its way to the US East Coast, the ship sunk
carrying California gold ingots and nuggets.*

As Good as Gold

ot everyone was cut out for mining. Few
understood how hard the work was until
they actually toiled in the gold fields. By late 1849,
there were so many miners working in California's
Central Valley that finding a fruitful area in which

to search for gold became more difficult with each passing day.

For many gold seekers, it was hard to concede failure—most never struck it rich in the gold fields. The journey to California had been a long, expensive trip—all for nothing. Too exhausted and broke to make the return trip right away, hard-luck gold miners turned to what they did best to make money—the jobs they had done back home. Because so many men were trying their luck in gold country, numerous jobs in California went unfilled and many services failed to be provided. Lumber, for instance, was needed to build houses, but no one was available to run the sawmills or drive the wagons to deliver wood. Some of the failed gold miners had done these jobs back East and found that people in California were willing to pay good money to get this work done.

Doctors, who had given up practices in their hometowns, returned to medicine and filled a desperate need for physicians in San Francisco and in the mining

The End of the Rush

Historians have not assigned an exact date to when the California gold rush came to an end. Most agree that it occurred in the winter of 1855–1856. By then, most of the easily accessible gold had been mined and individual miners were replaced by large gold-mining companies. Mining continued and money was still being made, but the hysteria was gone.

towns. Tailors, bakers, butchers, cooks, carpenters, and merchants were all needed to help build and maintain the rapidly growing cities of San Francisco and Sacramento. Because of the serious lack of housing on the West Coast, builders were needed to construct boardinghouses and hotels. Others were hired to run the businesses. Even the simplest things, such as washing bed linens, needed tending to and required workers to provide travelers with clean, fresh hotel lodgings. Those who turned to jobs other than gold mining eventually developed California's economic base and mapped out the future of California's cities.

Women in the Forefront

Though greatly outnumbered, women made California a livable place for the swarms of newcomers. As missionaries, teachers, owners of boardinghouses, and temperance speakers, they saw the need for and helped organize civic groups, schools, restaurants, and houses of worship. They pushed for the construction of roads, sidewalks, and sanitation facilities.

When gold seekers first arrived in San Francisco, the streets were mostly mud holes. Garbage was thrown everywhere. The city was infested with rats, and rat-hunting dogs were brought in to control the rodent population. People paid as much as $20 ($522 in 2010 currency) to get a cat to keep rats out of their wooden shack, tent, or cabin. Women tried to bring cleanliness to San Francisco and some of the mining towns by pushing for more sanitary conditions, including cleaning clothes and organizing ways of disposing of garbage other than throwing it in the middle of a road.

Luzena Wilson arrived in gold country from Missouri in 1849 with her husband, Mason, and two small children. Mason was certain he would strike

Mail Call

Next to gold, a letter from home was one of the most precious commodities of the day. These letters lessened the homesickness that spread throughout most of the mining towns. Lonely and discouraged miners waited for these letters, which were often accompanied by hometown newspapers.

In the early days of the gold rush, there was no mail delivery service in the West. Miners had to go to post offices, which were few and far between, to get their mail. In 1849, a post office opened in Coloma. So many miners waited for mail that they formed lines as long as half a mile (0.8 km) outside the post office.

Forty-niner John Durivage said that not getting a letter from home was "more depressing than the actual possession of evil tidings."[1] Realizing the miners' hunger for mail gave William Brown, who had no success as a miner, an idea. He put together a route and started delivering mail to camps for a fee. He made more money in a week delivering between 500 and 600 letters than he did over four months panning for gold.

gold; Luzena was not as confident. After Mason put up a campsite, he went off to the gold fields. Luzena got busy making biscuits for her family's dinner. The aroma of the homemade baked goods filled the air and a hungry, scruffy-looking miner followed the scent to the Wilsons' campsite. He offered Luzena five dollars ($131 in 2010 currency) for the biscuits. Shocked, Luzena did not know what to say. When the miner did not receive an answer, he upped his offer to ten dollars ($262 in 2010 currency). She took the money. She then purchased two boards and built a table. Within hours, Luzena was serving dinner to 20 miners. She charged a fair price and maintained a clean kitchen. The Wilsons quickly made enough money to open a hotel in Sacramento, called the El Dorado, striking gold a different way.

Gold Sparks the Entrepreneurial Spirit

All types of businesses had opened in San Francisco and throughout gold country. Food was in great demand and many who found mining too difficult used the rich California soil to grow crops to feed the influx of miners. The forty-niners also needed transportation, and several enterprising young men opened ranches where they sold everything from wagons and harnesses to horses and mules. Some miners left the gold fields for greener pastures in the entertainment field. They built theaters and brought in singers, dancers, and actors to stage plays. They then started vying for their share of the riches by selling tickets to entertainment-starved miners.

Levi Strauss built his fortune in California gold country on a pair of pants. In 1852, 23-year-old Strauss sailed from New York City to San Francisco to open a branch of his family's dry goods store. He brought with him some heavy canvas material. When the ship docked, Strauss walked along the San Francisco water front and was stopped by a miner who inquired about the material. The miner was impressed with how heavy the material was and commented that it would make a great pair of pants. The miner told Strauss that pants

Pay Dirt

Plenty of money had been made in the California gold fields. In 1849, $10 million ($261 million in 2010 currency) worth of gold was dug out. That was an enormous amount at a time when the nation's entire federal budget for that year was $45 million ($1.2 billion in 2010 currency). The amount of gold mined sharply increased to $41 million ($1 billion in 2010 currency) in 1850, and soared to $75 million ($2 billion in 2010 currency) in 1851. The amount of gold pulled out of the California countryside hit an all-time high in 1852 at $81 million ($2.1 billion in 2010 currency).

wore out quickly in gold country. No material could survive the wear and tear in the gold fields.

Strauss designed a pair of pants with the material, reinforcing the seams with copper rivets. He dyed the material blue, and the pants became known as blue jeans. Strauss eventually used a denim material to make the pants that the miners referred to simply as Levi's. By the end of the century, Strauss had a large plant in San Francisco that employed 500 workers to make the pants. His company's annual sales exceeded $1 million ($26 million in 2010 currency).

In 1852, Philip Armour walked from New York City to California. When he arrived after the six-month hike, he worked as a miner and dug ditches in Placerville to earn enough money to start a butcher shop. He did a booming business. Five years later, he moved to Milwaukee, Wisconsin, and used his savings to build the meatpacking empire Armour & Co.

John Studebaker, a wheelbarrow maker, had been a wagon maker in Indiana. With his move to California, he built a large clientele in Placerville. After working out West for five years, he took his savings and returned home. He started a carriage works business with his brothers that eventually became the Studebaker Automobile Company.

Levi Strauss in the 1850s

The gold rush had an impact far beyond making California the thirty-first state. It had an impact on the entire country. People earned enough money in the gold rush to start new businesses throughout

A Song and a Banjo

An untold enemy in the mining towns was boredom. When miners were not working, there was little to do. Some creative fortune hunters used their downtime to write lyrics about gold mining and living out West. Some set the lyrics to popular tunes of the time, such as Stephen Foster's "Oh, Susannah" and the British nursery rhyme "Pop Goes the Weasel." Original tunes included "The Fools of '49" And "Sweet Betsey from Pike." In the evenings, when it was too dark and raw to hunt for gold, talented miners grabbed a banjo, sat outside their tent, and sang their songs for anyone who gathered to listen.

the nation. The population growth in the West sparked the growth of the steamship business for mail in 1848 and for passengers by 1849. The population growth spurred the beginning of construction for the first transcontinental railroad. The New York to San Francisco link was completed in 1861. As the population increased, it created the need for the Pony Express and the expansion of telegraph lines. It prompted the nation to find ways of bringing the same goods and services that were available in the East to the West. The gold rush made the West grow fast. It made pioneers and adventurers out of many easterners and gave the United States one of the most colorful and exciting periods in its history.

Chinese laborers followed the rail layers to space and spike the rails for the western link of the Transcontinental Railroad.

TIMELINE

1848	1848	1848
On January 24, James Wilson Marshall discovers gold at Sutter's Mill in Coloma, California.	On January 28, Marshall informs John Sutter about the gold discovery.	On January 29, Sutter asks his sawmill workers not to say anything about the gold discovery.

1848	1848	1848
On May 12, Samuel Brannan runs through the streets of San Francisco, proclaiming gold has been found in Coloma.	California's military governor, Colonel Richard B. Mason, visits the gold fields in June and makes a report to President James K. Polk.	On August 19, the *New York Herald* is the first major East Coast newspaper to report the discovery of gold in California.

1848

On February 2, the treaty ending the Mexican-American War cedes California to the United States.

1848

The first rocker is used in the California gold fields on March 9.

1848

On March 15, the *Californian* newspaper reports the discovery of gold in California's Central Valley.

1848

John Sutter Jr. arrives from Switzerland in September to help his father save his property and to begin planning the future city of Sacramento.

1848

On December 5, President Polk addresses Congress and confirms gold is in California's Central Valley.

1849

In April, forty-niners descend on Missouri to start the overland trip to California's gold fields.

TIMELINE

1849	1849	1849
On September 1, the California Constitutional Convention convenes.	By the end of the year, more than 500 ships made the Cape Horn sea route to California.	By the end of the year, 90,000 gold seekers had come to California.

1851	1851	1852
By January, surface gold is disappearing.	The California State Legislature repeals the Foreign Miners Tax on March 14.	Hydraulic mining is used for the first time in California gold rush country.

1850	1850	1850
The California State Legislature passes the Foreign Miners Tax on April 13.	On May 19, foreign miners rebel against the monthly tax levied against them.	California is admitted as the thirty-first state in the Union on September 9.

1852	1852	1856
On May 4, a new Foreign Miners Tax is enacted by California's legislature.	The amount of gold mined hits an all-time high.	While gold mining continues, the period known as the California gold rush draws to a close.

ESSENTIAL FACTS

DATE OF EVENT

1848–1856

PLACE OF EVENT

California's Central Valley

KEY PLAYERS

❖ James Wilson Marshall
❖ John Augustus Sutter
❖ Samuel Brannan
❖ Jennie Wimmer
❖ James K. Polk, US president
❖ Colonel Richard B. Mason, US military governor of California
❖ Forty-niners

Highlights of Event

❖ James Wilson Marshall discovered gold in the American River in Coloma, California, on January 24, 1848.

❖ Samuel Brannan, a newspaper publisher, ran through the streets of San Francisco on May 12, 1848, confirming that he saw the gold in Coloma.

❖ President Polk addressed Congress on December 5, 1848, and detailed how plentiful the gold was in California.

❖ In April 1849, gold seekers headed to California by wagon train. The California newcomers became known as forty-niners.

❖ By the end of 1849, approximately 90,000 people migrated to California.

❖ Gold country suffered from many social ills, including disease, lack of housing, discrimination, environmental devastation, and crime.

❖ California became the thirty-first US state in September 1850.

❖ Many gold seekers failed at mining but succeeded in other business ventures.

❖ California's population soared to 300,000 by 1854.

❖ By the winter of 1856, the easily accessible gold had been picked clean. The rush to riches in the California gold fields was considered over, bringing a close to the gold rush era.

Quote

"The accounts of the abundance of gold in that territory are of such an extraordinary character as would scarcely command belief were they not corroborated by the authentic reports of officers in the public service who visited the mineral district and derived the facts which they detail from personal observation."—*James K. Polk, US president, December 5, 1848*

Glossary

alloy
A mixture of a precious metal, such as gold, with elements other than the metal itself.

amalgam
A blend or mixture, usually of metals.

Anglo
A white American of non-Hispanic origin.

boomtown
A frontier town that is quickly built.

cede
To give to.

discount
To not believe or to disregard.

dredge
To pull up soil from a riverbed or streambed, which often causes serious environmental damage.

immoral
Conflicting with traditionally held principles.

influx
Coming in.

insatiable
Unable to be satisfied.

lease
A contract that specifies the time and cost of renting something.

lye
A substance that can destroy or eat away by a chemical reaction.

malleable
The ability to be shaped.

mercury
A silver-white metallic element.

onslaught
> People arriving in huge numbers.

pay dirt
> Gravel, sand, or soil with gold in it; having success at some venture.

pristine
> Unspoiled, untouched.

prospector
> A person who pans for gold.

public domain
> Not privately owned; in the public sector.

rancid
> Rotten.

recoup
> Reclaim, get back.

sophisticated
> Complex or refined.

tailrace
> A waterway used to carry wastewater away from a mill.

topography
> The physical configuration of a piece of land.

vigilante
> An individual who seeks out justice on his or her own terms by avenging crimes.

ADDITIONAL RESOURCES

SELECTED BIBLIOGRAPHY

Brands, H. W. *The Age of Gold: The California Gold Rush and the New American Dream.* New York: Doubleday, 2002. Print.

Merry, Robert W. *A Country of Vast Designs: James K. Polk, the Mexican War and the Conquest of the American Continent.* New York: Simon, 2009. Print.

Rohrbough, Malcolm J. *Days of Gold: The California Gold Rush and the American Nation.* Los Angeles: California UP, 1997. Print.

Woodworth, Steven E. *Manifest Destinies: America's Westward Expansion and the Road to the Civil War.* New York: Knopf, 2010. Print.

FURTHER READINGS

Richards, Leonard L. *The California Gold Rush and the Coming of the Civil War.* New York: Knopf, 2007. Print.

Walker, Dale L. *Eldorado: The California Gold Rush.* New York: Doherty, 2003. Print.

Web Links

To learn more about the California gold rush, visit ABDO Publishing Company online at **www.abdopublishing.com**. Web sites about the California gold rush are featured on our Book Links page. These links are routinely monitored and updated to provide the most current information available.

Places to Visit

Empire Mine State Historic Park
10791 East Empire Street, Grass Valley, California 95945
530-273-8522
www.empiremine.org
This park is the site of one of the state's oldest and richest hard-rock mines. Tour a museum that houses a model showing the extensive inner workings of the mine. Some of the minerals found in the mine are also on display.

Marshall Gold Discovery State Historic Park
In Coloma on Highway 49 between Placerville and Auburn
530-622-3470
www.coloma.com/gold/marshall-park.php
Visit the site of Sutter's Mill where gold was first discovered in 1848. It is also the burial site of James Wilson Marshall.

Sutter's Fort
2701 L Street, Sacramento, California 95816-5613
916-445-4422
www.nps.gov/cali/planyourvisit/site10.htm
Visit the site of Sutter's Fort where many of the original buildings have been restored. Artifacts from the gold rush days are on display.

SOURCE NOTES

Chapter 1. Eureka!

1. Paul Walker. *Trail of the Wild West*. Washington, DC. National Geographic Books, 1997. Print. 15.

2. Liza Ketchum. *The Gold Rush*. New York: Brown, 1996. Print. 1.

Chapter 2. Word Gets Out

1. American Guide Series. *California: A Guide to the Golden State*. New York: Hasting, 2001/1939. Print. 71.

2. Dale L. Walker. *Eldorado: The California Gold Rush*. New York: Doherty, 2003. Print. 79.

3. Ibid. 92.

Chapter 3. Rush to Riches

1. Peter Browning. *To the Golden Shore: America goes to California—1849*. Lafayette, CA: N.p., 1995. Print. 36.

Chapter 4. Westward Ho!

1. Twyman Osmand Abbott. *A Treastise on Probate Law and Practice*. San Francisco: Electrotype, 1904. Print. 26.

2. Gary Kinder. *Ship of Gold in the Deep Blue Sea*. New York: Grove, 1998. Print. 7.

Chapter 5. Perils at Sea
    1. Liza Ketchum. *The Gold Rush*. New York: Brown, 1996. Print. 27.

Chapter 6. A Long, Unforgiving Trail
    1. Laurence I. Seidman. *The Fools of '49: The California Gold Rush 1848–1856*. New York: Knopf, 1976. Print. 72.
    2. Ibid. 74.

Chapter 7. Culture of Hatred
    1. Donald Dale Jackson. *Gold Dust*. New York: Knopf, 1980. Print. 74.
    2. Ibid.
    3. Liza Ketchum. *The Gold Rush*. New York: Brown, 1996. Print. 46.
    4. Laurence I. Seidman. *The Fools of '49: The California Gold Rush 1848–1856*. New York: Knopf, 1976. Print. 192.

SOURCE NOTES CONTINUED

Chapter 8. Sins of Gold Country

1. Malcolm J. Rohrbough. *Days of Gold: The California Gold Rush and the American Nation.* Los Angeles: California UP, 1997. Print. 147.

Chapter 9. As Good as Gold

1. Donald Dale Jackson. *Gold Dust.* New York: Knopf, 1980. Print. 228.

INDEX

Index Continued

Sacramento, 10, 23, 30, 44, 88, 90
Sacramento valley, 10, 30, 78
Saint Joseph, Missouri, 57
Saint Louis, Missouri, 9, 57
San Francisco, California, 9, 10, 23, 24, 26, 27, 39, 40, 44, 48–50, 52–54, 59, 67, 83, 84, 87–92, 94
Sawyer, Lorenzo, 79
Scientific American, 50
sea voyage, 42, 48–52
Sherman, William Tecumseh, 28
Sierra Nevada Mountains, 13, 63, 64, 80
Siskiyou Trail, 31
slavery, 8, 48, 52
sluice, 80
South America, 31, 40, 48, 50
Strauss, Levi, 91–92
Studebaker, John, 92
Sutter, Johann (John) August, 9, 10, 12, 16–18, 21–23, 30, 64, 72
Sutter, John Jr., 30
Sutter's Fort, 10, 12, 13, 17, 23, 30, 64
Sutter's Mill, 10–13, 14, 17, 18, 21–22, 23, 28, 31
Sutterville, 30

tailrace, 12–13
Taylor, Zachary, 37
Texas, 19, 20, 37, 38, 39
Thomas, William, 50
transcontinental railroad, 94
Tyler, John, 37

United States Magazine and Democratic Review, 38
Utah, 20
Utah Territory, 7

War Department, US, 32
Washington, 37, 39
Washington DC, 32, 59
westward expansion, 36–40
Willamette valley, Oregon, 31
Wilson, Luzena and Mason, 89–90
Wimmer,
  Jennie, 13, 14
  Peter, 13
Wyoming, 37

Yerba Buena, 9

About the Author

Robert Grayson is an award-winning former daily newspaper reporter and the author of books for young adults. Throughout his journalism career, Grayson has written stories about athletes, arts, entertainment, business, politics, and pets, which have appeared in national and regional publications, including the *New York Yankees* magazine and *NBA Hoop*. He has written biographies of environmental activists and professional sports figures as well as books about animals in the military, animal performers, law enforcement, and major historical events.

Photo Credits

AP Images, cover, 3, 6, 15, 16, 19, 25, 65, 69, 75, 76, 85, 86, 95; Library of Congress, 11, 26, 35, 36, 45; Getty Images, 33, 55, 66, 82, 93; Picture History, 43; N.Currier/Library of Congress, 46; Alamy, 56, 58